TOP 10 MOVIE HITS

10 of the Most Popular Melodies from the Silver Screen
Arranged for Late Intermediate Pianists

Sharon Aaronson

Top 10 Movie Hits are among the most popular songs from films during the 20th century. This collection of all-time favorites spans a wide variety of genres, from animated feature films (Walt Disney's *101 Dalmatians* and *Aladdin*), actual movie themes (*The Pink Panther* and *Theme from New York, New York*), and music from movie soundtracks (*Can You Read My Mind?*, *Over the Rainbow*, *The Man That Got Away* and *The Wind Beneath My Wings*). The two earliest pieces in this collection, *As Time Goes By* and *It Had to Be You*, achieved new life when featured in the movies *Casablanca* and *When Harry Met Sally*. Whether a fan of classic or current films, this collection is sure to appeal to today's performers.

I was thrilled to have the opportunity to work with this wonderful music. I hope that you find as much pleasure performing these pieces as I did in arranging them for you.

Sharon Aaronson

to Sandi and Bobby, with love

Copyright © MMVIII by Alfred Publishing Co., Inc.
All rights reserved. Printed in USA.
ISBN-10: 0-7390-4633-0
ISBN-13: 978-7390-4633-3

As Time Goes By

(from *Casablanca*)

Words and Music by Herman Hupfeld
Arr. by Sharon Aaronson

* Optional.

Cruella De Vil

(from Walt Disney's *101 Dalmatians*)

Words and Music by Mel Leven
Arr. by Sharon Aaronson

Can You Read My Mind?

(Love Theme from *Superman*)

Words by Leslie Bricusse
Music by **JOHN WILLIAMS**
Arr. by Sharon Aaronson

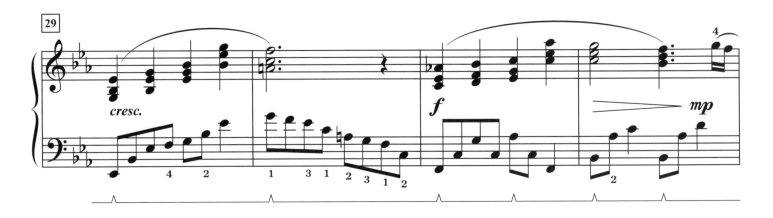

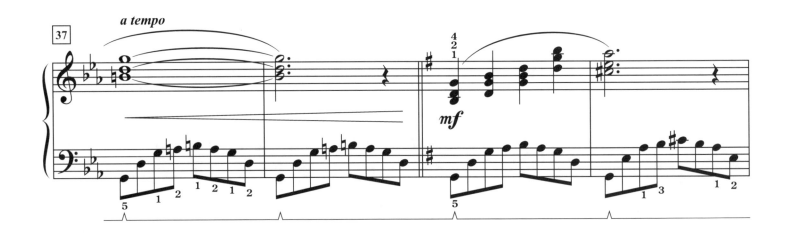

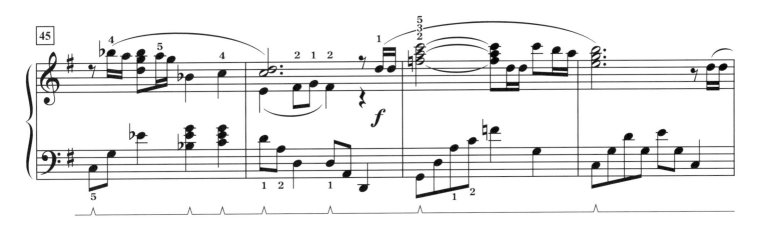

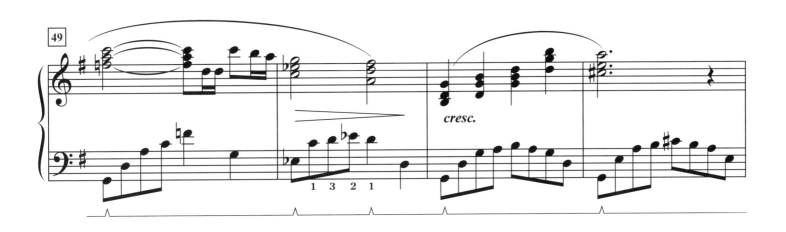

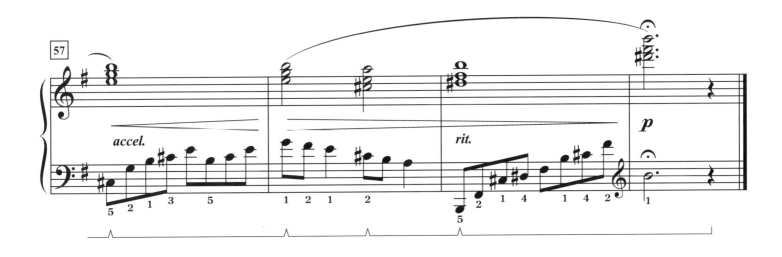

It Had to Be You

(as featured in *When Harry Met Sally*)

Words by Gus Kahn
Music by Isham Jones
Arr. by Sharon Aaronson

Over the Rainbow

(from *The Wizard of Oz*)

Lyrics by E. Y. Harburg
Music by Harold Arlen
Arr. by Sharon Aaronson

The Man That Got Away

(from *A Star Is Born*)

Words by Ira Gershwin
Music by Harold Arlen
Arr. by Sharon Aaronson

Slowly and expressively, with much rubato

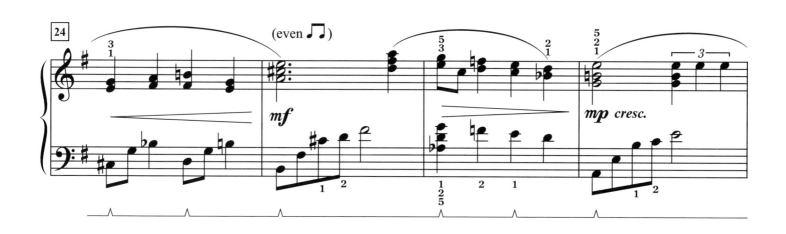

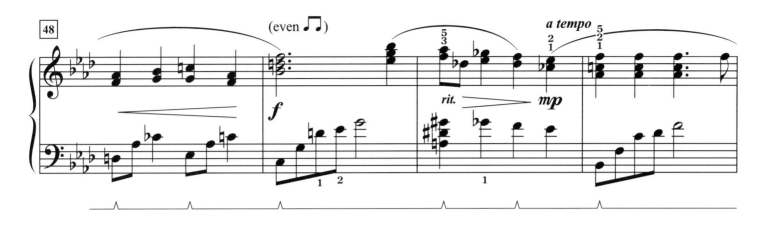

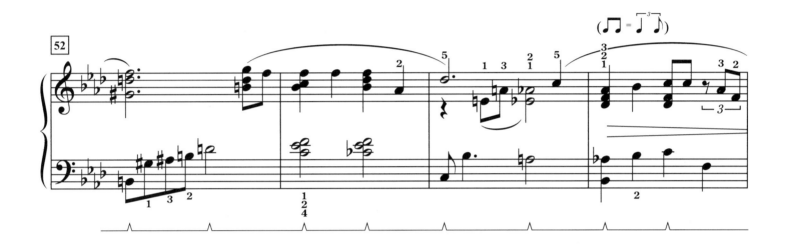

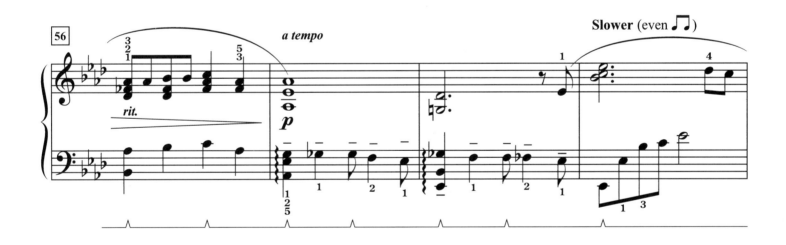

The Pink Panther

(from *The Pink Panther*)

Music by Henry Mancini
Arr. by Sharon Aaronson

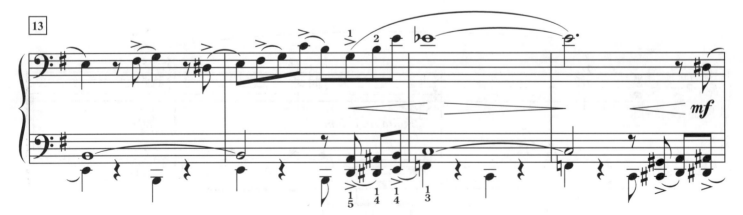

A Whole New World

(from Walt Disney's *Aladdin*)

Words by Tim Rice
Music by Alan Menken
Arr. by Sharon Aaronson

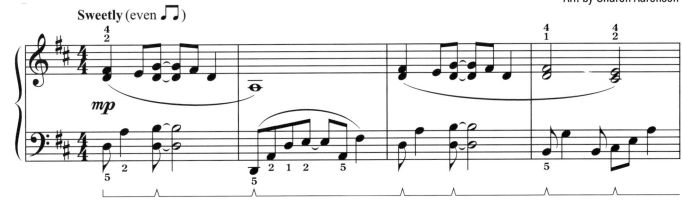

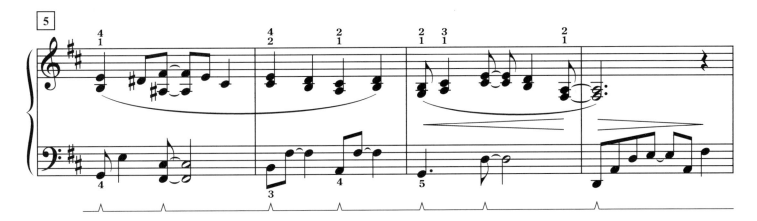

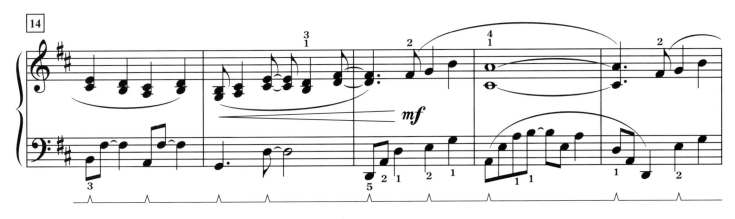

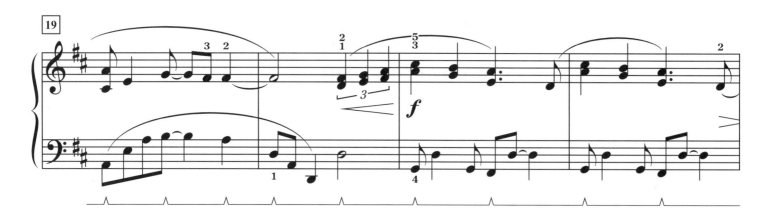

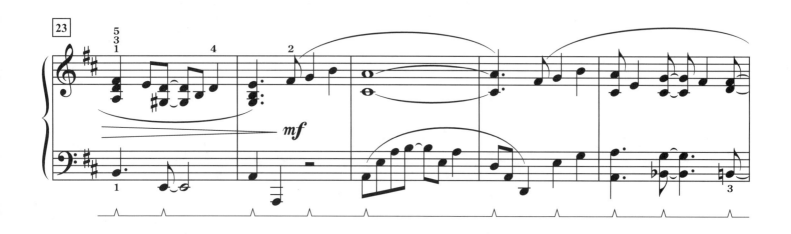

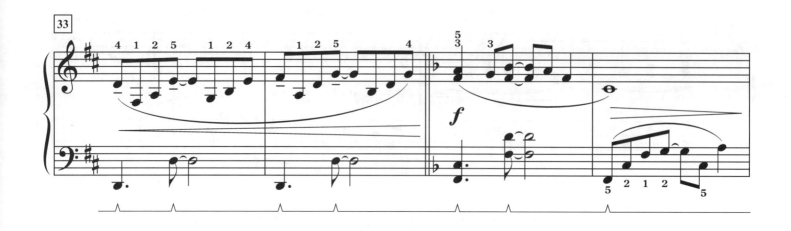

Theme from *New York, New York*

Words by Fred Ebb
Music by John Kander
Arr. by Sharon Aaronson

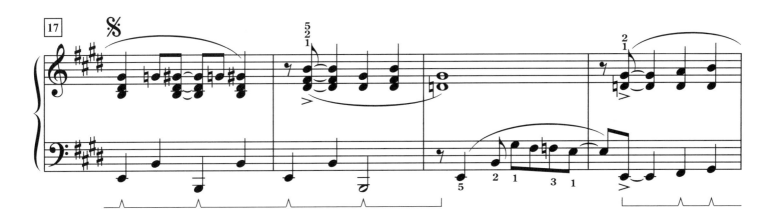

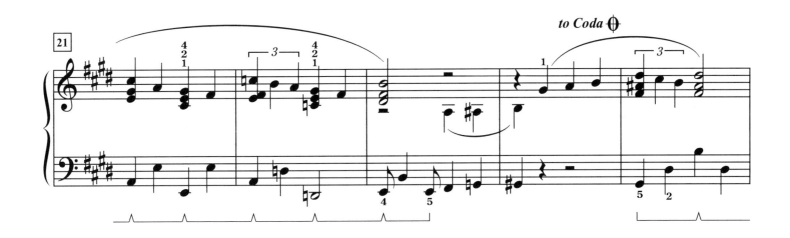

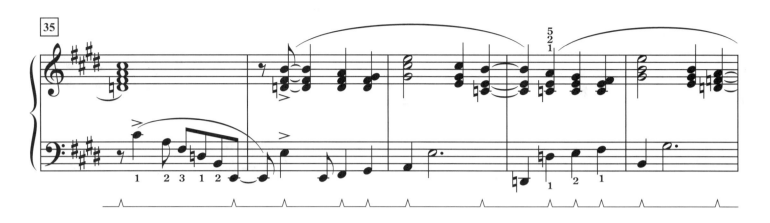

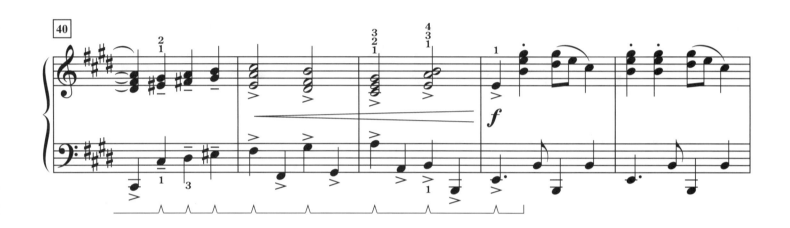

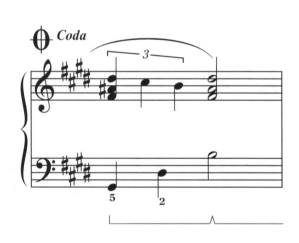

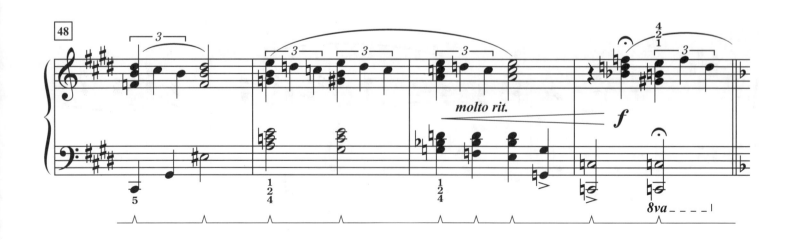

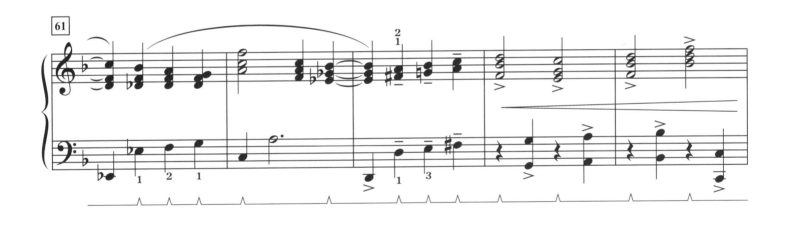

The Wind Beneath My Wings

(from *Beaches*)

Words and Music by
Larry Henley and Jeff Silbar
Arr. by Sharon Aaronson

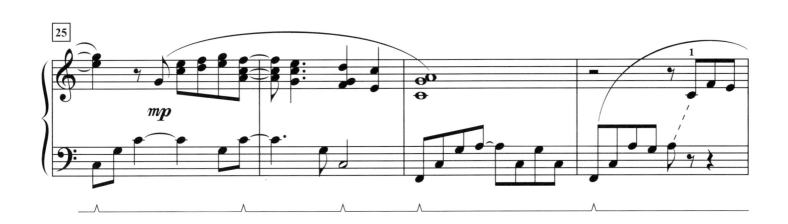

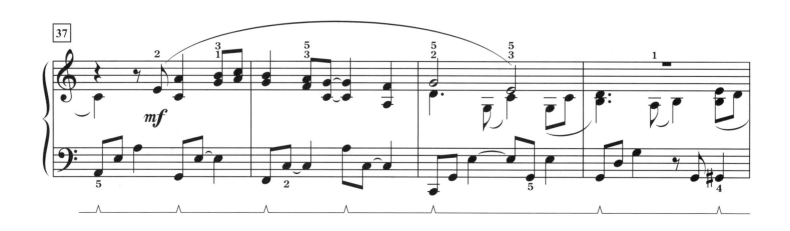

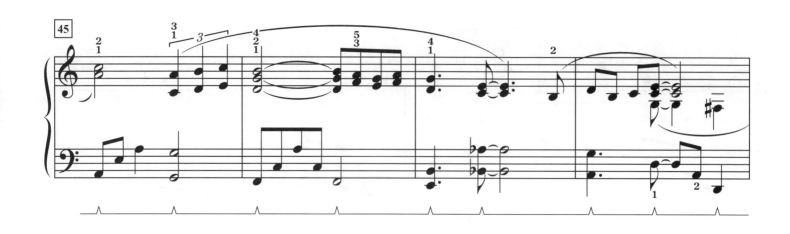